THE BLUES COLLECTION

By

JACOB LEWIS

BLACK BOX PUBLICATIONS

Copyright Jacob Lewis, 2007

The right of Jacob Lewis to be identified as the author of this work has been asserted in accordance with the Copyright, Designs and Patents Act 1988.

ISBN – 13: 978-1-906374-00-6

A CIP record for this title is available from the British Library.

Published by Black Box Publications.

Printed in England by CPI Bookmarque, Croydon

SETLIST

1. Suspicion is warranted
2. Purchase no.1
3. Entelechy
4. A Prayer for my Dad
5. A relatively short Doctor Doctor joke
6. California never killed anyone
7. Brokedown Wetherspoons Blues
8. How to hold a woman, lessons 5, 6 & 13
9. Mysterions
10. Divorce Petition
11. Joshua, by proxy
12. I want my children to grow up to the sound of canned laughter
13. The circuit
14. A choir
15. We are young
16. Orpheus lighting up
17. A polite reminder
18. Power suits your eyes
19. Early Warning System
20. Nuclear family

Suspicion is warranted

found a dead boy in a crater
at the bottom of my garden
brought him back to life with
green tea and Mozart and affection
called him Alex
after the great conqueror
taught him everything I know
he didn't do well at school
showed no sign of super powers
I carried him on my back
until he was 14
because his spine was weak
and he was prone to blackouts
which shook my world
because I didn't know how
long they'd last.

Alex had a breakdown at 21
I told him where he came from
showed him the exact spot
by that point I loved him
felt he was mine
so I tried to infuse the story
with the same tenderness that
mothers fill the bellies of storks
or priests feed their manger - dreams
but it was no good
I couldn't patch him together
he wanted to know
I don't blame him
he tore up the garden
looking for clues

found only memories
i'd given him
a punctured football
hacksaw blades coins
bucket and spade
a cut knee
that made him hate me
thought I was covering up
he searched the internet
for other dead boys
and conspiracy stories
went missing for a week
I got the shakes
couldn't concentrate at all
drank too much
waited for the police to call
didn't do the laundry

when he came back
he said he understood
wouldn't explain
but said sorry
said no more worries
would ever come our way
said it like a prophet
like he had super powers.

we lived together
for 20 more years
can't tell you how happy we were
measure it in oceans instead of streams
skyscrapers instead of bungalows
not everyone is allowed to love
remember that.

when I died
he cried until his eyes
became earth - dry
he howled and screamed
until his voice left him
he beat his hands against
the walls of our house
smashed them into mulch.

that night
he dug a giant hole in the garden
laid me out
assembled all of my favourite things
around me
waited for me to return
but I never did
not once
no matter how hard I tried.

Purchase no.1

You bought yourself a tiger
For security
For the hallway
Partly because it was the fashion
That Indian Summer
And partly because if
Like people said
You really did
Need a man around the house
To protect you,
You figured he should
At the very least
Have sharp teeth and claws.

Your first choice was an albino
because you thought it would
blend in better with your blonde hair
and minimalist space – age flat
but they were all sold out
so you had to make do with the normal kind.

The little bastards in the marketplace loved it
like you knew they would;
animals built for killing
are impressive to a young mind;
they lowered their hoods and scowls,
as respectful as monks,
and after a while of petting it
began to understand
as much about its beauty as its violence,
which was quite upsetting for those
who had put all their faith in the latter.

Your tiger became a regular feature on our street
much loved and respected
although some bitter souls
whispered every now and again
that when you were lonely
you let it into your bed,
and if it did paw the odd person here and there,
the police took the long view
and let you off with a warning.

Now it's old like you
and doesn't carry the same threat,
when it growls
it sounds like a polite complaint
Rather than a command,
but I think by this point
everyone has got the message
that you want to be left alone.

Wasn't that the message?
I hope so.

Entelechy

Our kid grows in the next room
the girl we never had
the one we never thought about
until it was all over

she's in the vase of garage flowers,
in the wheat yellow carpet,
in the flat pack furniture and the
whirring breathing sound of the boiler.

everything precious in the next room
signifying peacetime.

A Prayer for my Dad

My father was a chat show host
and every morning at breakfast,
he would talk to us two about
how we were feeling,
our lessons at primary school and
whether we'd met anyone special yet.

He'd be waiting there for
a good hour before we got to the table,
dressed in a powder blue suit,
a moon white shirt with silver cufflinks,
shiny shoes and a shiny smile,
benign posture and second – hand thatched hair.

We were understanding children
so we tried to answer his questions clearly,
allowing him time to make jokes,
sometimes at his expense and
sometimes at ours,
and when we told him stories
about our more dangerous scrapes,
he seemed particularly pleased,
glancing occasionally out of the window
for signs of approval,
as if he thought there might be
some flaw in the morning sky,
a mark that the Gods might need entertainment
in the same way we need water.

By the time we got to school,
we felt like superstars.

My father was a seventies astronaut
back when being a space invader meant something,
and every morning at breakfast,
wearing his full NASA gear because he never
knew when that call from abroad might come,
he would talk to us two about
our dreams and aspirations and what
we wanted to be when we grew up.

Our mum left when we were infants,
frustrated by the fact our father was more
interested in the New Scientist and weather reports
than making love on a sheepskin rug
or holidaying in the South of France;

without her by his side,
we thought he probably wanted to leave too
but that wasn't practical or legal,
so instead he would disappear for weeks on end,
which for an astronaut probably
feels like a few dream – like minutes,
but for us was a starvation, a landslide.

My father was a magician
and every morning at breakfast,
he would flounce in wearing a black cloak
to our hammed - up shock and awe
and proceed to produce a full spread:
buttered toast from thin air,
a boiled egg from each sleeve and
orange juice blown out of a straw until
our glasses were full to overflowing.

It didn't matter that for some years
we'd been able to see through the gaps
in his tricks, because that meant
we were becoming magicians too
and as adults would practice the same tricks
to even greater acclaim,
with even more glamorous assistants,
because we would be better magicians,
never relying on the same play twice,
and would keep our children at a respectful distance
so that they wouldn't see the illusion at all.

My father was a cowboy, a soldier, a spy.
My father was a boxer, a movie star, a fireman

and every morning at breakfast he would

he would

forever and ever

Amen.

A relatively short Doctor Doctor joke

Our great and gracious queen Victoria
has set up a suicide stall
at the back of Camden Lock Market
doling out kindnesses at five quid a shot.

She says, All Pills are Good,
It's just situations that turn from good to grim,
quicker than golden bank holiday Mondays
turn into leaden office hours,
situations that turn as sour
as charity misplaced on street corners
or rainwater on a commuter's back,
and sometimes, she says, sometimes
there really is nowhere to hide
except medicine.

She's got sauce, though,
comes across like a nu – age Charon,
joss sticks drawn at dawn,
still mends her tights of an evening,
and sings Russian folk songs quite out of tune
when you least expect it,
but she's not quite so equitable
When it comes to party treats.

Sure, it's okay if you're over 50 and terminal
but when the young boys with sweat quiffs
lunatic hearts and soft hands
and the girls with no brakes
and hair the colour - mix
of sawdust and black coffee;

when they come to ask her
for the power to forget
she turns them back kindly,
says suicide is not the answer,
that they've fallen in love
with the packaging and
not the souls trapped inside,
so she takes their phone numbers
mixes them up in a hat
and then gives them back out.

That's our Queen Victoria:
part death's head,
part fortune teller
and part dating agency.

That's not to say she lacks heart,
that if she refuses someone,
she doesn't scan the tabloids the next day
with thin, worried fingers bronzed with nicotine

to find stories
or half - stories

of the woman drowned in the Thames
with a bellyful of baby parts,
or the guy with the superfly style
but an accidental and absolute conscience.

What really worries her, though, is when
they throw a fresh new copper
on to the streets of North London;

A bloke walking on the dark side of the moon
with a few quid and a tazer gun in his pocket;

because that sort of thing
becomes a self fulfilling prophecy,
you know?

So she sits them down early doors and
knowing full well it could go either way,
she says to them:

Love gets overwhelmed by experience

Listen to what I say

It happens every time

You may think this job is your life right now
but love always loses out to experience.

She tells them about the good ones
who are long gone,
retraces the lines of tragedy
until they thicken, deepen and then shadow,
And hopes that they know someone
who knows someone
who needs to join the others,

and if she has one eye on the exit herself,
the 100 meters dash to a taxi cab,
while a fellow market stall owner
provides a violent distraction,
who can blame her?

California never killed anyone

When people say casually
they wish they'd been alive
in the sixties
they mean acid, free love,
rock and roll without the money
ruining every groove,
a world less confused,
a clear space away from
dismal and clammy hearts,
they mean
some hope in a better future -
that maybe if it was them
with their shoulder
at the wheel back then
it might have turned out differently.

this girl I like
she has the same rationale
only connect
as a romantic
but she takes it to include killing, torture,
and the training of young men
not to freeze when met by a boy
or a woman who pose a threat,
however slim.

when I say I wish I was alive in
the sixties the fifties forties thirties
it's because I want to know who I am
outside of the loop
I want to know how well
I would have taken orders

how dishonest I would have been in
any given circumstance
whether history would have flooded through me
to the point where I lost perspective.

I already know the answer,
so the desire itself is something akin
to having blood on my hands,
something I used to worry about a lot
until I worked out that I was no - one special.

Brokedown Wetherspoons Blues

The Italian is telling us his life secrets,
all of them, in some detail,
and the Afghan soldier sitting next to me
glazes over because he's of the
opinion that everyone has their own tragedy,
in his case burying his child
and having to kill people who were once friends,
in my case an addiction to reality teevee
and an ex - wife lost somewhere in the USA.

We're both wearing suits while
the Italian unburdens himself
because we've just finished for the day
at the law firm we work at,
me as an ambulance chaser
and him as a translator and fixer.
The suits and our silence and
the Afghan's discursive smile lends
the whole scene a psychoanalytical feel,
even though all three of us
are drunk enough to jump up
and sing Sinatra at the drop of a hat.

When I look over at him,
the Afghan raises an eyebrow
in comradeship and I smirk back;
he's got his religion to keep him warm at night
and I've got my cynicism to do the same.
He makes friends easily in the UK because
there's a rhythm to the way he speaks,
a slow symbolic self - mythology,
that and his visceral hatred of neo - cons,

his distrust of technology
and the fact he doesn't complain
when he gets stopped at Heathrow.

The Italian says that his mother
tortured him with an electric cable
and a screwdriver.

I don't know what he
means and I don't want to know,
so I excuse myself
and go to the toilet.
I have a line for a poem
that might go somewhere,
so I walk quickly.

"do you lie when you dream?"

I keep on saying it over and over again
because I don't want to lose it
and maybe I think
owning this valuable knowledge
makes me different
than all of the other people lurching
in and out of the pub

Do you lie when you dream?
Do you lie when you....
Do you lie when you dream?
Do you dream when you....
Do you...
Do you lie?

How to hold a woman, lessons 5, 6 and 13

This is easy
your hand lies on her hip
her back curls into your body
and the warmth of the bed
was waiting for you
when you opened your eyes
so this is instinctive
and because you don't know
if it's love now or ever or anymore
you slow your breathing and heartbeat
so that they match hers.

she says: are you awake?
and maybe she's scared
you're ill or weakening
but you don't answer
and she goes back to sleep.

This one is cut and paste
nothing you can do
she sees shadows under your eyes
and around your jaw
that she attributes to bankruptcy
of one sort or another
and now she wants out
so when you hold her
it's temporary
it's still and quiet and complicated
like a diagram explaining how
to put together an airplane
so you're aware that this is a memory
before you even close your eyes and move in.

she explains to you
in a subdued voice
the difference between
love and lust.

I ask her what she plans to do
when her sexuality runs out?

This is the most difficult manouvre
take the cigarette out of her mouth
one arm raised to gather up her shoulders
you have to be strong
and her weak
contrary to real life
think about dancing slow dancing
when dancing meant freedom
and the rustle of her skirt
and the kiss of her skin
against your body
made you an artist
made you an architect
able to build a metropolis
from a few small scraps of time.

Will you let me stay here
for the rest of my life?
she said
will you hold me when I'm
less vivid, less beautiful?

I say in the past
you wouldn't even have asked.

Mysterions

Angel's a performance artist in the
small blue - light clubs around north London,
the kind of places that open up when
the theme pubs have let out their steam,
when everyone real is shuffling home
and there's nowhere else to go.

She comes on in-between
the acoustic complainers
and the twist
introduces herself as just another Angel
and brings out a razorblade,
cuts her arms through her clothes and
lets it bleed for about five minutes,
and then walks off
through the cheering crowd.

She's got dark hair and a pretty pale face
so the goths claim her as one of their own

She stays silent when she performs
so the cool kids nod along

She's got no idea of fashion
so the intellectuals applaud smoothly

and then she walks off
through the cheering crowd

She hasn't read a book since GSCE level
so the extroverts whoop and yelp

She looks as empty as a wooden bowl
so the druggies feel a kinship.

She's got good gams and a nice rack
so the loaded lads lap it up

and then she walks off
into the cheering crowd

My friend James caught her after a show once
and pretended to be a journalist,
half from that sallow kind of satire
that all sharp smart young men
hold so tightly to their hearts,
half because he wanted to know if
she was mad
before he asked her out on a date.

He bought her a double Jack and coke
from the hard faced Polish girl at the bar
and while the blood dried
on her yellow silk shirt,
he asked her whether she wanted to be
a nurse when she was growing up.

It's a line he uses with every girl
and it seemed particularly apt for Angel
but she didn't bite,
telling him her life-story
with all the glamour of
a butcher giving up a old cut of meat,
about how she used to be an office worker
selling equity release plans to oh ay pees
but three months in it started to go wrong

because she would bring in random objects
and put them on her desk
just to liven up the day
cocktail shakers elaborate illustrated candles
pictures of long dead movie cowboys
until her workspace was a home from home
and how when she was given a formal warning
about her behaviour, she draped
a dead chicken over her computer monitor
and dared them to fire her.

She told him she still wasn't sure if her life
might not be one giant breakdown
waiting to happen,
that the scarred walls of her body might mean
that one day she would drive
her car into a crowd of children
outside a school
or else cause her to take flight
from the genius height of a skyscraper
but for now
while these eager little signs of madness
glint like gold
she wants to entertain you
although she hopes that one day
her skin won't bleed so easily.

My friend went home with her phone number
and an open invitation to see the show again,
but I think he'd seen enough.

Divorce Petition

in luton - london,
I went to the doctor regularly
with back problems
to get you happy pills

in ann arbour,
we talked about how chinese students
would take over the world
in ten or fifteen years
and how it was probably for the best.

In madrid,
we thought we saw flashes of fascism
in cinema staff
but chose to blame it on the weather.

in bercy,
listening to animals getting strangled
in the night,
i pretended to like your mother

in chicago,
you sneaked me into your feminist college
so we could fuck and smoke
and drink cherry vodka.

in swindon,
I bought you a paper moon
for a 100 watt bulb that blinded us
but you junked my present
on the grounds of taste.

in hawaii,
we spent $100.00 on cab rides
and then argued over whether we
could afford to order pizza.

in amsterdam,
we lived for a week off
your tenuous connection to a dead rock star
and found out that the Dutch
like to drink and talk during movies.

in pontiac, MI,
i danced in the car-park of hospital
and from the 4th floor you waved
and blew kisses
while the black orderlies smoking outside
applauded and sniggered.

in london,
i'm living your dream
drinking and joking with thieves and murderers
and drag acts and chefs and poets,
some of whom will remember my name the
following morning

I'm not sure what happened to my dreams.

in london,
i've missed you,
but no more than usual
and I don't
answer your emails anymore.

Joshua, by proxy

You gave it to him, didn't you?

there was something
passed down in the blood
while he was breathing inside you,
a poison that stopped him from growing
and made his bones weaker than papier-mâché,
alone in the crib
weighed down with sticks and stones.

maybe he knows his name already
maybe it's sunk in
maybe he senses something is wrong

you wanted a forceful boy but he'll
change his mind, mid - sentence:
you know the type
you wanted a lion but you got a Christian

maybe you should go to Spain
because they don't know you there
neither of you have a history
and the truth is every place in Europe
is the same now
his heart would harden in the heat
and you could meet a different type of man
who wouldn't mind the odd accident
here or there.

You can sit out on the veranda
with a margarita and a bottle of tablets
and cough sweets
and snooze in the mid afternoon
measuring time in years not days.

the only problem is that food spoils
much quicker out there
and when it rains,
it really does rain.

I want my children to grow up to the sound of canned laughter

At nine o clock Greenwich Mean Time
somewhere West of Shepherd's Bush,
we get into a drunken conversation
Tayo, Ridley and me
about which country in the world
is the most corrupt.

we're all qualified in our own way
to pass judgment

Ridley is a solicitor advocate
due next week in the Sudan
to help the poor Africans out
with their legal system,
a sweet bald guy in this thirties
who would like to be a record producer,
a re-occurring dream, I've noticed,
of men my age and class.

I've burned him a DVD
with the full Chess Collection
and the new Springsteen
because he's going to the bad part
of the Sudan in the hope of
getting a plush UN job nine months later.
He tells me it's a two day drive
to the European quarter, where
they have bars, libraries and safe women,
so he's going to have a lot of
time and repression on his hands.

Tayo is a young Nigerian
who works in the same firm
on less important immigration cases,
those people who have little or no
chance of success,
life long unrepentant PKK members,
Australian actresses who forgot to
return back home on time,
Turkish men who are running
from the bird flu and
Chinese couples who claim to be dissidents
but run at the first sign of ghosts.

Me?

I'm a solicitor and a sociopath,
but one who knows a lot of
influential people in low places.

For the record,
Ridley went for Russia,
Tayo for her home country,
and I said Kashmir,
but I was voted down
because it's still considered a war zone
and they don't count.

So I went with Nigeria too
because my uncle has
spent most of his life out there
getting kidnapped and bribing officials,
selling black on white porn, booze
and Shirley Bassey CDs to the natives.

we laughed, got more drunk,
but we knew the real results:
there's an official corruption index
run by the Germans
who were considered the best people for the job
as they believe in Government
above all else.

For all you pedants in the arena,
the Winner is Chad.
I repeat: Chad.
Shame on you, Chad.
There'll be no lottery money
from me next time.

Later on two Saudi businessmen
offer to double my wage if I come
out to work for them
because they like the look of my face.

I say no, I'm happy with the UK,
eleventh in the index,
historically prone to
long distance warmongering,
but somewhere I can bring up my children
safe in the knowledge that bombs
are dropping everywhere else but here.

The Circuit

jack and blue are huddled in the corner
starring in their own homemade movie;
she's celebrating a dearly beloved uncle
who just died of boredom,
leaving a grand after tax and black box costs,
while he celebrates the blood in his piss,
because it means 28 points for sure
and a life of fine and overeasy leisure.

pam suggests we spring
the Holy Ghost out of wormwood scrubs

he's been in there for far too long
for a crime we all still joke about,
so she jumps up and down on the bed
until we agree to follow her plan:

she wants to lean ladders up
against every wall in the universe
so every boy and girl alike
can fuck up their own small piece of freedom
in their own sweet way.

john is drawing chalk outlines on the wall
for long lost friends
and tells us in a voice of pure reason
to wind us up
that Judas was a fighter prince
a bar brawler with a mouthful of broken teeth
and that if Hitler were to ever
set up another comeback tour
he could fill Vegas ten times over.

karen's in the bathroom
giving head to some German guy
she met at a festival for old punks,
so I guess their second date is going well.

Alison is chatting up kid Lancelot
by listening to his problems.

he says that when technology improves,
his true love will come back to him.

most of the time, Ally doesn't know
whether to kiss the boy
or administer last rites,
so she settles for somewhere in between.

amy salts the carpet
to make sure nothing grows tonight
but she needn't worry:
nothing grows around here.

she offers me a halo made out of foil.

she says I deserve it for the bruises on my arm
and the glint of green in my grey eyes.

I ask her what time her heart is at,
lifting up her skirt.

she says she's just hit midnight
but she's racing faster than police cars,
losing forty minutes for every hour.

she says she's shaking through the world

so fast that she'll rip into the morning
before the sun even yawns.

I scream into her face,
grind my teeth,
open my mouth so widely that my
jaw splashes splinters against my collarbone
while I chatter obscenities
as loud as I can into the deep of her shell - like.

I'm going to drown before you,
I shout at her over the scuzz of noise,
it's a competition
and I'm going to get there first.
I can feel it.
lay money on it.
lay money on it now.
please. please.
now.

she just laughs at me and
turns up the thermostat.

A choir

The subject comes up of babies,
which has become a real problem lately
since the immigration department moved from
their own offices in Wood Green to ours,
bringing with them a crowd of applicants
who want to stay in the country
despite the best advices of our Government,
and often arriving with their children.

One of the immigration solicitors says
we should stick them out with the bikes
or put gaffer tape over their mouths,
because he thinks it shows a lack of respect
if you take a scowling bawling infant
with you to seek professional advice.

The Indian woman from Accounts
calls him a Scrooge
because it's ten days to Christmas
and points out that sometimes
you can't get a family member
to babysit at short notice.
She loves children
more than anyone else
because the medical profession have
concluded that she can't have any.

One of the personal injury solicitors
says in response that immigration clients
always seem to bring their
entire fucking family with them.

I stay quiet but my own feeling
is that people keep their family close
at these impossible times
to show an unanimous front,
like when in their own country
they might go to plead a case in numbers,
but also out of fear that their relative might
get scooted away at any given moment.

Immigration is poorly paid and relies on
idealists working long hours

The boundaries of countries are
retraced every day.

Client are routinely asked
to deny their heritage
through fixed - fee translators.

I don't know.
Maybe I'm as racist as the rest of them and
I'm looking for something that isn't there,
but I do like to hear
the sound of babies in an office
because they make me feel alive
when I feel at my most death - like.

The solicitor who deals with
multi - million pound clinical negligence claims
says we should open up a crèche
and make some money out of them.
Everyone seems to agree.

We are young

two o clock in the morning with Ariel and
still going strong on vodka and
cigarettes and flirting and
half - chewed theories about right and wrong,
me on the side of the angels
and her somewhere in between,
she tells me about Alex,
her first boyfriend at school,
who told her that when he reached
the age of twenty he'd kill himself
because he didn't understand what
the point of life was,
other than some abstract throwing up of meaning
that wouldn't even convince an infant,
the sun, the moon and the stars,
or three black rectangles on a red background,
it was all rubbish according to Alex,
trivia for the damned.

So on his twentieth birthday,
he hired a room in a city hotel
and hung himself. She wasn't going
out with him by then, but
remembered his promise and stayed in
that night, hoping the telephone
wouldn't ring.

pass the bottle, she said,
because I need to toast him right now
for teaching me something about life
that otherwise I wouldn't have understood,
because after months and months of crying,

cursing him for staining me
and thinking about it so incessantly
that my head felt trapped in a vice,
I came to the conclusion that you can't
save another person if they want to go,
no matter how much you love them
or want to protect them,
because not every cry is a plea for help,
not everyone is settled inside their identity
or senses a moral structure
in the solid redbrick of their family home
or the shadow of a local church
and when all of the glasses are collected
in a gasp and a rattle at the end of the night
and when opinions fade away,
we should grip on to our existence
with both hands,
however painful and bloody that might be
because it's a long, long way down,
so far that we can
no longer see ourselves
when we're down there.

I put my arm around her and mumbled
a few drunken words of consolation,
my sex still potent between my legs,
but she looked straight through me,
as if I was just another stray
walking through her memories.

Orpheus lighting up

this man was found dead back in June
with snow and Christmas lights in his hair
sitting against an allotment fence
no witness except
a scarecrow with its back turned.

no - one around here knows who he is
but we're trying to find his relatives
as best we can -
the posters have gone up
and there's talk of a radio advert
in the next few weeks.

In the evenings,
children run from door to door
to tell everyone the news afresh.

someone said he killed himself
over a good - looking woman

someone else said that there was an
avalanche of ravens from the sky
that fell into a single spot on the earth
and into that pool of wings and eyes and beaks
he walked downwards into rapture.

someone else said he looked like a druggie
the type that drinks straight from the bottle
hangs around in shopping malls
to secretly film women
and is barred from every pub from
here to Hades.

We'll probably never find out
but that's no reason to stop trying.

A polite reminder

I caught you looking old
the other day.

Don't ever let me see you
do that again.

Power suits your eyes

This morning
I woke up to find
a midget with blue hair
jumping up and down
on my chest
his small furious feet
hoping to stamp me
down into my bed - grave
while he screamed out insults
in a foreign language.

The midgets are always in the front line.
Expendable sporty Napoleonic.
Small blunt instruments.

I was expecting something like this to happen
ever since I wrote an article
in the local newspaper
warning about the dangers of
letting the circus come to town.

It starts out innocently at first,
fliers the colour of strawberry and cream
promising extravagant women and animals,
the kind of happy danger
that shies away from the more
traditional Friday night joys of
a beer bottle to the scalp
or rolling around in the gutter
with a needle quiet in your arm.

But wipe the glitter out of your eyes, people,
because I've seen what happens
in other villages and towns
when you let the carnies take over
because they never really leave
and for every citizen who wants to run away
ten freaks want to find a home.

The local girls already dream of far – off places
and need no encouragement to fall in love with
the Boy Magicians and their smooth girlish hands,
to find warmth and consolation in the Ink Snake
draped over the Strongman's upper body
or the escape artist who slips in and out of
bedroom windows with the greatest of ease,
as thin as an exclamation mark.

Do you really want these false gods
roaming the land?

A dead elephant sits in the corner of your room
largely unnoticed.

Surly clowns gloom around dole offices,
hoping to make a sideways move
into IT, PR work or market research,
face paint darkened around their mouths
from the sheer volume of fake cigar explosions.

Dancing girls with gynecological kinks
offer cash in hand services
of the kind which would
turn any good man to dough.

On pure statistical evidence, more young children
Disappear from supermarkets on circus days.

I know a friend who broke her little toe
When an acrobat landed on her.

I know another friend who's seen human bones
In the big cat cage.

All I'm asking is:
think carefully before you jump.

You've spent so long making this town
in your own image:
why throw it all away on
the need to be different?

Early Warning System

I don't know where I got the lump from
maybe from the IT Department
they seemed really scared about the Y2K bug
then there was the I love you virus
and the problem with a bad Windows disk
which turned out to be relatively small.

I'm going live now.

I'm going to show the world my lump
and I hope that all of the most important
people of my generation turn up to watch.

I don't want anyone to see it as a striptease
it's important I get my message across
but I have to accept that foreign audiences
those who live in a primal state of television
or the tramps who stand outside electrical shops
will mistake anything colourful for heat.

When I was younger,
my fear of mortality was so strong
that I wanted everyone to go with me
that was the only way I could face it
and how my teachers spoke about
the environment and nuclear war and AIDS,
I didn't think I'd
have to wait this long.

Do you have similar memories?
There'll be a number for you to phone
if you do.

Now it's come, finally,
it seems laugh out loud humorous
that as the make - up lady
puts magic tape on my breasts
makes my lashes longer
and plumps up my hair
puts blusher on my lump
to make sure it shows up
under the squinting star - shaped lights
that the one thing now
I need everyone to know
is that I'm alone,
that no matter how many people
I collected as friends
or loved as more,
whether they let me speak tonight or not,
or how glam I come across,
that they understand
this death is mine
and only mine
to distribute as I wish.

Nuclear family

My mum is famous in our house.

Dad caught her out in a lie
and now we're wondering
where it'll end.

I take photographs of her
like it's glamorous
while my brother Alan sits crying
in the comfortable chair
as if somebody shot the princess.

Mum hides behind the door,
the way famous people do
to avoid unwanted attention.

the red light on the DVD player
is clicking on and off
with a pathological joy
and only Dad knows how to fix it.

He's out hunting other lies.

He doesn't know if it's big game yet
or sweet little nothings
and although he carries himself
in the same way as normal
logical hopeful exemplary
it's like the sunshine
has been scrubbed out of him,
because he never wanted to be famous.

Detective

It's 2 am and the cold night air creeps up my back,
stealing warmth from whatever it can hold on to,
but it can hold nothing, gather nothing, and drifts
like any other jilted lover with no place to settle.

And another Brixton Jesus is calling down the apocalypse
from the safety of a bus shelter,
screaming black and blue murder
to raise his voice above the sound of the hooves
clattering on the top of the roof
and the taunts of day – glo clubbers slouching home.

Me, I specialize in smaller disasters:
dismal marriages, rent repossessions,
drug addictions, that sort of thing,
a geologist of sorts, plowing the South of the City
for the shells of those hollowed out by their past,
working on prosaic signs and signals,
disheveled gardens, boarded up windows,
discarded prams and mattresses;
investing in tired faces and dropped postures,
in the sweet memories that have atrophied over
the long haul from debit to credit to nowhere.

It goes without saying that London
is the best city in the world for this type of work -
the weather passes into the back of your mind
and remains there, waiting for a sign of weakness,
eking out a confession from the part of you that still cares,
while you go about your day to day.

3 am comes and the clouds open up as predicted,
the rain invading everything,
laying a curtain over the architecture
until the clean hard lines of every building
cede into a softer haze,
recreating the world as I would want it,
in my own vague image.

And on a night like this,
if you were to ask me if I feel sorry
for the characters that I collect, I would tell you:
no, only for those who joy in the hardness of this town,
who cheer the way it makes strangers out of good people
and Gods out of pieces of tinsel and glass,
because it's better to have sinned and lost, my brother,
than to have never have sinned at all, better to
have loved the wrong person than the wrong world,
better to die with blood on your hands
than with a dead heart.

All lies, of course.

The answer changes depending on who is listening.

Cities are built on echoes, not original truth,
however far back you care to reach.

B MOVIE ACTOR

I know the limits of my world now,
the black and white frames clattering
forward like train carriages,
casting out a montage of wartime glamour,
young American soldiers with big bustling shoulders
sucking on cigarettes as if they were baby bottles,
the busy lobby of a liberated luxury hotel,
a touch of silk on a long slim leg
dangling over the side of a bed.

The war has been over for a long time, of course,
and all of the extras who cluster at the edges
of the screen like bats, filling up the empty
spaces in picture and plot, are long since dead;
like me, they never quite moved on to starring roles
or took control of the whole damn beautiful show,
and as a result, while you watch them,
their blank, stilted expressions roar with white noise.

It's nearly my turn to step up, and
I feel raw and clumsy because
the flowers in my hand are shopworn, wilting, and
everyone knows that she will turn me down again.
Did she love me once?
Did she ever wake up shouting my name?
Her face looks similar to someone I once cared for
and I try my best to pretend, like the others do.

Golden

The love which I once took for granted
is no longer so certain,
and I dread the coming of Autumn,
that melancholy, disheveled season.

That was when we first met,
and as each year passes,
and they seem more and more
like laps of the same circuit,
I realize that if there is a natural end,
it is closer to the heart of that season
than any compact, or place, or tide.

And it is at moments like this
I wonder where I found the capacity
for thinking in such grand and emotional terms,
and I realize afresh with some depression,
and not a little horror
that I must have learnt it from you.

The Box

I wrote this poem to break your heart,
to cause you a permanent wound,
but it was already broken, with the pieces
hidden from me in old haunts, better memories,
the distance between my feelings and yours.

So I re - wrote this poem to get over you,
better to talk you down to others
and tell the story with retrospective grace
so that the next one would think I stand whole,
but it was also no use,
because you kept on returning,
in one way or another,
and there was no room for others.

So I changed this poem so I could trace my way
back through fingerprints, openings, hopes,
to find out why this still means so much to me,
but the marks I found, they faded as I wrote.

So I changed this poem one last time
to fill in that emptiness where
all of my old lovers remain,
still loved, so that the next one
wouldn't feel that sadness,
but she read these lines and understood them
better than I ever could, anxious and shaking
in front of the bathroom mirror the next morning,
hungry to chase down her own past.

So I wrote this poem as a requiem of sorts
in the wish that one day you might open it
in your hands and know that I still miss you,
but the song went wasted, its longing quieter
than the crowd at the boundaries of your life.
So I finished this poem,
but found that it like you had changed over time
and was now more like a toy than a real thing,
to be put away in the attic
with all my other forget me nots,
where it sits still.

Master and Servant

He dreamt he shot some people
in the fruit section of a supermarket,
but in fact he saw only the aftermath,
a row of dead bodies wrapped in clingfilm
as if awaiting shipment,
his shaking hand dropping a gun to the floor,
the trays full to bursting with melons
and pears and kiwi fruit,
and, at some point,
an excitable crowd cheering
for a sluice of blood.

Later on that night
he found the same bodies again
but this time in Eastern Europe
after the interment of a mass grave,
leaning up against each other
to form chevrons pointing skywards,
but he is not able to talk to them or point
out where they might have gone wrong,
only walk around and watch
the reactions of the liberating soldiers,
some weeping without restraint,
others despairing in silence,
while those with harder hearts or darker humour
take photographs of themselves by the empty hole
like proud amateur gardeners or ironic tourists.

Later on that same night
he has an asthma attack
his lungs locking up, grinding shut,
and the intense panic waking him
to find a forest of infants sitting around
and on his bed, crowding at his body
and sticking their tiny fists inside
his mouth to choke him.

His Body's Response

When it came, he was not surprised
or frightened, taking in the bad news
like someone reading about a
foreign disaster in the newspaper,
horrified but attached at a distance,
drawing the picture from a quieter shore,
the opened letter on the blue and white
striped kitchen table like a torn white sail
on placid waters, the contents opened and read,
then replaced with a smile to his wife,
his every activity casual but wakeful,
while his body became more and more diffuse
to the point where he felt forced, cheated,
into picking up his fresh tea and drinking it
to burn the light pink inside his mouth
and visit the safety of its quiet ache.

He liked to call it his great project,
more out of humour than pride,
but the strength that had hauled them out
of the deep vindictive mines of his youth
meant as much to him as it ever did,
though the history of his skin and musculature
was definite now, no longer open to interpretation,
because in the tight arches of his stiff form,
the physical mannerisms,
a snowy white slosh of hair,
his loved ones perceived the landscape from
which they had grown.

When he told her, three days later,
she wanted nothing else but to comfort him,
and he said to his wife in response, weeping,
letting go for the first time in thirty years of
marriage:

Please hold me. Not just my body,
but me.

and he hoped that she understood.

All Breakages Have To Be Paid For

Grant is a sweet romantic with sharkish teeth,
a body that falls under the tube train every night
rumbling and random with deviant lingo,
supermarket booze and good clean dust,
but clamouring for that something holy,
that something essential he finds
in the clarity of the sharp labels
he wears with casual glamorous force,
in the donor card resting snugly in his pocket,
in the girl who stands around the next corner
waiting to sweep him off his feet,
and in the tall lush grin brimming
with kissie-kiss celebrity
he flashes as he strolls into the small cafe,
where everyone is his friend because
everyone is his friend.

And he feels joy in the company of strangers
because fame is cheap in the terminal drag and
every visit is nostalgia even though he never left,
but where he can meet questioning eyes with
something approaching affection because he
can say honestly he has never lost himself
in the hatred of another human being, never harmed
another soul without first harming his own,
and never let truth get in the way of love.

Amy won't live through the next few hours
but she's going down fighting,
spitting out the dirt and blood
from an earlier burial as she tries to
catch up with her soul, that dull muggy

shape that's been two steps ahead of her
since she was a child, but the hallelujah
lies stale on her purple painted swollen lips
and the markings on her body tell a
different story, a black butterfly crippled on
her upper back and three light scars
on her left wrist like military insignia.

And she feels comfort in the company of strangers,
who, like her, look out of place in their own lives,
but two hours have passed since she first entered
the cafe, with only a salmon paste sandwich
and a mug of tea to show for her rent,
and the shift workers seem to bristle at the
dear charity of keeping her alive, upright,
the small cluster of workmen in their thin
luminous yellow coats and green hard hats
crowded around a table towards the back,
emanating miserable solidarity, deep dunking
their biscuits as if mining for precious elements,
while a policeman at another table makes
everyone nervous, his laughable attempt at flat
anonymity betrayed by a pair of listless eyes
which periodically sweep the shop, his actions
like a painting in a haunted house.

Bry got the cancer vote a few seasons ago,
so he sleeps one night out of three and walks
the streets in the space in between, shuffling
past the hushed up sunken buildings
with a flask of coffee under his arm and
a kitchen knife strapped to his leg,
hoping to find a number or word that seems
out of place, some accidental clue or sign,

that will give him meaning and lessen the hunger
of his dreams, those strange aquatic scenes
in which the sites of his pain match
the coloured dye that pushes out into the water,
blue for his shoulder
red for his hip
yellow for his eyes
and black for his mouth.

And he feels safe in the company of strangers
because as he passes the small cafe
and sees the steam welling up at the window and
takes the thuggish smell of heaped
fried chicken into his nose and his gut,
it feels like an invitation back into life
without reservation or even interest,
a place where the weight can slip off him
like a gown, where he can leave his death mask
at the counter in rough, disinterested hands,
and where he can scatter the lilies behind
him like so much waste, the flowers he collects
in every hospital waiting room,
but he is stopped at the door
by a girl who smiles up at him,
her head resting on a shoulder
made soft and clumsy by the drunkenness
of her boyfriend,
his daughter too late
his wife too soon
his girlfriend smiling
and the place is suddenly too close to home
for him to stay a minute longer.

Frannie is brittle, a record that got part - wiped

somewhere between the hesitant twitch of the
long hand at twelve and the harder line at two
that supports her heart like a prop, the party
that began a day ago now sunken into spare change
and the last empty chair
in a cramped Turkish cafe in Leytonstowe,
the stiff piped heat gluey on her skin
as she sits drinking cold coffee while drumming out
a low hypnotic beat against her ear
to stop the moon, stars and concrete
from spilling out of her head and over the table,
the raw material of memory turned over to
the beautiful untranslatable, too precious to share.

And she feels kinship in the company of strangers
each crashing at their own pace,
tired rushed words circulating in the air, a
steady stream like the grey protective hum of transit,
because everyone is a stowaway at this hour,
the night keeping sleepers soundless safe,
but blowing the rest ragged and restless
into the bare-backed morning.

Absence and Illness

There's a man burning on the factory floor
and it's not even half past nine.

John at table three was the first to notice
but he was too scared to put things right
and rather than extinguishing the fire, ran wildly
around the factory searching for an alarm.

David from the tech team was the next to notice.
He was outside snatching a quick fag,
but heard the screaming
and strolled over to the window
to see if he could be of any help;
a calm and practical dude, a big Elvis fan,
he crushed the ciggie under his foot,
sighed, and then headed straight inside,
covering the burning man with six or so coats
he grabbed from off the work hangers.

The rest of us had began to assemble by that time
and we watched him roll the guy around
until the last shards of fire were muffled into silence.

Sammy said I should go over and sit by him,
hold his hand and wish him well,
ease the loneliness of his last few moments,
but Sammy is a trainee like me and knows his place,
so even if there is some poetry left in his soul,
he doesn't move an inch unless ordered.

Virgil meanwhile kneels down to the body,
and looking over it with a heavy scrutiny
part medical and part religious,
he shakes his head slowly from side to side
and asks us if anyone knows the identity
of the dead man, but no – one comes forward
because the guy was part - time and kept to himself.

Virgil has joked in the past that such things
never usually happen before two o clock.
He's health and safety, so he ought to know,
but I'm never quite sure whether to take him
seriously or not, even now.

There *is* something in his manner
that makes me think he wants to protect us
but it often comes out all wrong, mocking,
malicious,
and I'm not sure if that's part of the training,
letting go, I mean, of the past and
letting sleeping dogs lie, whatever the circumstance.

He says people have more bravado after dinner time,
hyped up on sugary snacks and pies and caffeine
but it's false energy, so in time they roll around and
topple over like silent movie comedians.

I think Virge is crying.

Brian is the Manager of the factory
and from his separate office at the back,
he phones the top people at Bristol, and
although he tries to keep
his voice down, we all knew that he's

pleading for some sort of help.
The man's body is now lumped
and stripped of feature like a red raw thyroid,
the curious embers a dishonest sign of life.

David walks away from the rest of us
and phones the ambulance and police.
They come about fifteen minutes later
and take the body away, without query.

One by one we go back to work.

When I get home that night, I notice
a small black stain
on the hem of my coat, and
I'm forced to think briefly about the
events of the day again.

I wonder how it happened, about his family,
and whether he's the main wage earner.
I wonder whether his wife really loves him
like I think mine does most of the time,
and whether I'll be invited to the funeral.

Finally, I wonder whether something
like this will ever happen to me.
It's not likely, but who knows?

Art

At the tender, mixed up age of nineteen,
she began to collect broken men
for the fun of it, and at first it *was* a blast,
the energetic rush of divorcees, widows, and other sons
who had fallen by the wayside,
the betrayed, the forgotten and the mislaid,
romantics who had never dared to touch,
a host of crumpled souls from every corner of the
globe
flocking to her newly bought house in the Home Counties
in the hope of finding, finally, something sweet.

They wanted so much to be collected
that it was no effort at all, really,
but when her family and friends
worked out what was happening,
they crumbled away from her in horror and shame,
locking their doors, windows, and hearts,
pretending to be out whenever she came to call.

The men loved her, of course -
she had the classic fairytale combo
of beauty, purity and a good head of blonde hair,
though in truth it was not all one way,
each too in their own fashion
brought her something new,
if only for a moment,
some part of their sad history,
a snapshot of an old lover, real or imagined,
something made of silver or gold,
a gift or a prize or an artifact,
enough to keep them around

long after her attention had faltered
in the off chance they might surprise her again,
however unlikely that might be.

It was an addiction, you see,
that caused her to amass
these blasted and battered men
and stuff them into every nook and cranny of her house;
crushing them into spare rooms, cupboards and cabinets,
squeezing them into the garden shed
among the rakes and spades,
until the accumulation itself became her life,
and every door that she opened
caused hundreds of men to spill out.

But over time, her suitors grew suspicious,
exhausted from the bitter taste of desire half – met
and aware too that they were a collection of sorts,
that she treated it all like a game,
most evident in the lunatics tasks she asked of them,
like jumping up and down on her grandmother's grave,
or assembling for mock inspections in the back garden,
only to have her jump into their line,
knocking them over as if they were giant tin soldiers.

Gradually her collection, so closely arranged,
dropped to a few in number,
those awful men who were so lost
that they saw her as their final chance,
who scuttled around like spiders in the shadows of her skirt,
men so damaged, crooked and bent
that she could barely look at them without wincing.

She wished them away, then kissed them in the
hope that one might be a prince, but any such
hint of magic about them had long since gone
and they stayed resolutely ugly, disillusioned,
themselves.

That's the end of the story, such as it is,
because I finish where this collection does, and
although I wish I could give you more of a moral,
I'm afraid that I've looked the other way for so long,
hopeful that one day she might be interested again,
that I think I've already said too much.

Americana

I put a coin in the slot
and the shutter climbs up.

my baby is undressing behind the glass
a domestic scene
a full continental breakfast laid out
on a flower print tablecloth
while smokey robinson sings out from
a tinny sounding radio on the floor

I'm wearing a cowboy hat -
even though I hated Texas -
and a grimace I stole last gasp from
the body of a Manchester spinster

we never taught our daughters
to rock and roll
like we promised.

we didn't protect the rainforests
or even change to unleaded

we never conquered old age:
just look at the clouds in my hair,
the wrinkles that group and seem to
migrate towards the centre of my face.

just look at the blue in my eyes:
these stars have been broadcasting
their disappearance for some time

o, baby, we were always tourists.

False negatives

I was looking through the personal ads
for signs of life,
odd occupations and perverse body shapes,
women who admitted they were freaks,
references to bands I liked,
but in the end I was drawn to
a description that said simply
without plea or polish
I am the girl with the blurred face.

I wrote to her and
asked to see photographs
and she sent them
in their thousands;
I spread the small white - framed squares
over every point of my living room floor
and tried to work out who she was.

She had lived a grand life,
this girl with the blurred face,
equally at home
with the aristocracy as the plebs,
slouching through supper at the Ritz
or munching a pie of unknowable content
in Camden Lock Market;
there she was in wartime Paris,
her slim form at a balcony
pouring a cocktail into the crowd
to Christen the liberation;
there at the burial of a princess
and again at the birth of two children
from the same stalk,

there in a shop doorway rife with shadows
caught while kissing someone famous,
there at the fight where the boxer
hurt his shoulder and then his brain
and couldn't get back up again,
and there she was again, yesterday,
a few seats down from me on the tube.

She was everywhere and nowhere,
this girl with the blurred face,
so it made sense that she
was hiding in the anonymity of newsprint,
free from the attentions of a
a camera that seemed to transform her
into modern art at every new turn.

I took her on a picnic the following week,
a spread of Sushi, Haribo, Evian,
and the leftovers of the Summer Sun
laid out on a blanket in Regents Park.

I felt like hugging her
every time I looked into
that mess of colours and shapes and angles
where her features should have been
but I stopped myself,
afraid she might think it was sympathy
that made me want to hold her
but it was something far worse,
because I wanted her to be an outsider
so she could better empathize with me,
so she could stand by my side
on the periphery, looking in.

I guess I also read into her lack of features
or her excess of them
that dream - feeling I have occasionally
that the world must at some point
show itself on our bodies,
not like those adverts that purport
to show all - over skin cancer
or those that say autism
is a disease uniquely well - suited to our era,
not even like those parents
who colour - in and pierce their children
through a misplaced sense of tribe,
but some crack in reality
some whisper that cuts through the surface,
so that one day I might look down
and discover that my hands are made
of charcoal or marble
or find that the people around me
have forfeited the right
to see as clearly as they do,
and that many others are walking around
with their faces blurred.

But she wanted to be normal, this girl,
she wanted to live her life,
to take up all possibilities
and not swim in hypothetical waters,
so it was hardly a surprise when
she turned me down for a second date.

Reverse the charges

I woke up this morning with my double
laying naked next to me,
that fine upstanding man
who once tried to strangle my wife
and is rumoured to have
given a blow job to a grizzly bear.

his body is shaking,
his movements clumsy elephantine,
he's glued up with heart - sweat
but he calms down
when he sees me blink open.

I'd heard he was back
but it didn't bother me:
My people
they understand
it's understood
that we're strangers
and his business and mine
rarely connect.

I say double,
but he's suffered over the years;
he has a sour liver
from too many nights on the town,
his stomach takes on
another barrel ring each season,
his spine crunches when he walks,
his body angular
like a false celebrity shaken out
of cut - up magazine pieces,

and his greasy hair is limp and mopes
over his brow.

it's the best impression of a
shipwreck I think
I've ever seen.
Every time he turns up, I joke -
what have you done to my body this time?
show me something new
but this morning
is the first time he's answered me back

he said
this thing he said
it's a threat, I'm sure
"you should be more worried about
your memories, friend, not your body."

He's not much of a joker, my double,
but like I said
My people
they understand
it's understood
that we're strangers
and his business and mine
never connect.

sometimes I feel it when he gets hurt
no matter how far away
but I've never told him that.
Better to let him be a martyr
every time I bump my head or get a papercut
to justify the mess he's made of his life.

I promised him once that
if he was drowning, I'd save him,
and ever since he's been drowning.

There's a lesson to be learned there
but this isn't the place or time to learn it
and maybe I think there's promises
I've broken to decent people
that deserve a top class haunting.

I put my mouth over his
and we share a breath
the way we always do when we meet.

he takes what he needs
and I take what I need
the way we always do when we meet.

New and Improved

I saw the final cut of his new campaign
for Antovil, the painkiller to end all painkillers,
just legal enough to creep under the radar
but sufficient to whack out your granny
with enough left in the tank to do your
mum and sister too as collateral damage.

The advert was set in outer space,
a beautiful young woman floating outside
a silver ship shaped like a lipstick holder,
her face visible through the glass of the helmet,
but her hair plunged back into the darkness
to suggest the look of a newborn
grappling with the first moments of life,
an image strengthened by the stretched metallic
umbilical cord wriggling in the background,
detached from the place of her birth.

she breaks the silence,
whispering "it makes the pain go away."
and the picture turns white,
blotting out anything that might have gone before.

It's almost too easy to criticize the director,
a friend of mine, in fact,
with the reality of what happens next,
to try to imagine the pills
marching down a ramp like ants,
from the old woman in a rocking chair blissed out
to couples swapping educated silences,
from the high flying executive flying high
to young children sent to bed too early,

but the more I watch the advert,
the greater sense it makes to me,
that if the afterlife really is an empty sign,
or at least a space covered in scaffolding
and white sheets, awaiting a revamp for our era
that doesn't feel like a lie,
then all that does remain for now
is not to know, which I imagine
is a sweeter Heaven for most.

Fake Irish Pubs

speak low, my love,
now the working day is over
and the hours stand as dark
and burly as midlife brawlers,
the streets as empty as diagrams.

speak low, my love,
while we flicker at the bar like candlelight
and guess at the dreams of strangers
as they stumble or stab past us.

A man within earshot
presides in the corner booth
dressed in a shabby suit from the old country
and puffed up to the gills
with blue skies, good transport links,
dead kin and jar after jar of memory;

We listen for a while
to his stories and his songs
but don't join in with the crowd,
despite him calling us over
to fight the good fight
against the morning's call.

We speak low, my love,
while a girl leans against the travesty jukebox
dressed in pink corduroy and
a light spray of glitter on her face,
a lass looking towards the future,
to a sweet man and a kind house
in the suburbs,

to a place that knows no Winter,
looks forward to the prize,
to rows and rows of miniature luxury handbags
set out like urns in a family crypt.

speak low, my love,
and while we buckle but do not break,
let's talk about friends
who are long gone,
like old people talk about the war,
with a pea fog in our eyes
and a snarl of whisky and soda
to cushion the blow;

let's bring them back for one night only,
though they beat and blur
like ultrasound
and scare the children
enough to make them hide
behind lemonades and colas;
let's raise a glass to lost friends,
though they cause dogs to hiss and spit
at fallow walls and wet windows
and they forever fail to pay their tabs.

speak low, my love,
and let everything pass
while there's still time to forget,
still love enough for ceremony
in the play of our shaking hands,
our pale breath,
our drunk - epic smiles,
love for this stalled world we call home

Trust in me, the Autopilot

Mary and Dan arrived in London two years and one
bun in the oven later than planned and a credit card
debt that would've made even Atlas creak and bitch.

They were childhood sweethearts from up
Rotherham way, the result of a union between two
families that mixed like gas and flame; his half was
hand me down clothing, pub fights and scarecrow
meat, hers doilies, hand moisturizer and occasional
trips abroad.

She fell in love with him at the age of four
in the playground, when she caught
him trying to stare out a sunset
that the boy had somehow taken personally
and then wanted to capture.

He ran away before she
had a chance to tell him that
it was okay to back down now and again.

It took a further 8 years
before he took her seriously.

He was drowsy outside a local pub at the time.
She was whisper – thin, barely there, but with
a friendly familiar face.

His father, who had started him early on beer
and romance, told him:
"You make do with what you've got
and then you turn it into gold"

They rented the only place
they could afford in London.

Nobody has ever confused Camden with Paradise
but it was the best they could do, so they kitted it out
with cheap Moroccan cushions and wraps and
covered the walls with Picassos and pictures
of the New York Dolls before they got old and died.

Dan found some work as a council cleaner.
the pay was shit but they thought he was bright,
So they trained in the more technical stuff,
how to deal with deserted drug squats and dead dogs
and medical waste and neglected grandmothers.

Mary got a part time job in a club called the Wild
Palms where the men call the waitresses to their
tables with bells and whistles and cash in hand.

The owner was Northern
so he had a soft spot for her
and put her behind the bar,
safe from the fingers and thumbs of evil men
but not from their dreams.

She wore loose fitting dresses to hide her bump.
She smoked a lot of dope
To put things in perspective.

One night, when picking her up,
Dan broke a punter's nose.

He remembered a joke he heard
a few years back from his father
about what women will do for money
and he snapped.

He entered the man's head,
looked through his eyes,
saw the world as it really was.

She saw only the blood on his knuckles,
dinosaurs still roaming the earth.

That night, they chose the names
of their children-to-be,
counted them on their fingers –
one two three.

The following night Mary went missing.

Day Return

It's Sunday, 11 am, outside the St. Marcel Metro and
I'm one small bottle of wine down already;
Yellow in the gills and unsteady on my feet,
As vain, venal and cantankerous
As the ruins of Empire,
Blinking for air and
Praying that the roof of the world
Doesn't tilt down to say good morning
And rub me out for a sketch of a man.

By noon, I'm two small bottles of wine down and
Posing for photographs with Japanese tourists,
A smattering of French and German, a funeral –
Ready coat and a 2nd hand paperback novel
enough to convince them that I'm a native.

They've got one of those cameras that
Can read your thoughts, so every shot feels
Like a crime reconstruction.

By two o clock,
I'm three small bottles of wine down
And I fall in with some Afghan drifters
Who are getting high and drinking from
Brown paper bags and laughing at the
Parisians in the park with their
Ice – cream smiles and handbag dogs;
They smoke - snigger at the martial statues because
They've got war dead of their own back home
Who are measured in much smaller ways:
Unlocked doors, a few dollars, broken biscuits.
By the end of the hour,

They're laughing at me instead,
Because I'm tall and fuzzy like a dandelion clock,
And I'm trying to rub my last two memories together
In the hope I might find a spark.

At 3:30, a full moon is hoisted into the cool blue sky
And it fair breaks my heart -
It's like the rim of another glass raised to my lips,
Another pale cheek turned towards me.

At 5:00, I find an underground bar
Full of lonely girls in lonely dresses,
Sound tracked by Sinatra and Elvis and
Staffed with lazy Arab boys
Who were born on the make.

I drink for another couple of hours
And then stagger down into the toilets.
There's a African midget sitting in one of the basins
Gargling blood in his mouth and
Clinking around a mug full of donations.

I ask him if he can sing me a song while I'm pissing
And he tells me in broken English that I'm a virus,
A cancer on the world.

I tell him:
We've all got our own tragedies, son;
All of my cousins got blown into the wind last year,
So they're old newspaper now, biro scratches,
Out of date haircuts, coins on eyes,
Taken away dancing in stick thin arms.

It's just me left now
And if I'm a virus, my friend, a human cancer,
Then at least I outlasted all of the good people.

He takes a swing at me but misses.

I put my hands around his neck and squeeze
But run for the fire escape when he cries for help.

By 8:00, I'm back at the station
Looking for a fight with one of the
Many con – artists who lie in wait for
American faces and tumbledown baggage,
The kind of trickster that seems
To live and die in the flickering light,
Idly turning their pawn – shop wedding rings
Two clicks left and three clicks right,
As if trying to hit a perfect combination.

I trip one of them up with a low kick
And then run for the Eurostar,
Hearing the shouts chase me as I scarper.

I hide in the driver's section.
I hide in my hood.
I phone you.
I have kindness enough to tell you
I don't love you
And you have kindness enough
To stay knowing it.
I tell you:
If you don't want nightmares,
Stop dreaming, stay still, stay home.

You laugh. I cry.

Typical bloody scene.